Broken Vows
Crown of Splendor

Broken Vows
Crown of Splendor

Jillian St. James

Copyright

No part of this book may be reproduced or transmitted in any form or by any means, electronic or mechanical, including photocopying and recording, or by any information storage or retrieval system, except as may be expressly permitted in writing.

© 2009 by Jillian St. James

Jill Ink Press

ISBN: 978-0-9830352-7-5

Scripture taken from the HOLY BIBLE, NEW INTERNATIONAL VERSION ®. Copyright © 1973, 1978, 1984 by International Bible Society. Used by permission of Zondervan Publishing House. All rights reserved.

To order additional copies of this resource write: Jillian St. James at

brokenvowscrownofsplendor@gmail.com

Broken Vows
Crown of Splendor

You will be called a new name that the mouth of the Lord will bestow…a crown of splendor

Prologue

Oswald Chambers said, "At times God puts us through the discipline of darkness to teach us to heed Him. Songbirds are taught to sing in the dark, and we are put into the shadow of God's hand until we learn to hear Him... Watch where God puts you into darkness, and when you are there keep your mouth shut. Are you in the dark just now in your circumstances, or in your life with God? Then remain quiet... When you are in the dark, listen and God will give you a very precious message for someone else when you get into the light." Thus, *Broken Vows, Crown of Splendor* was written.

Contents

I. To Have and to Hold

II. For Better, For Worse

III. For Richer, For Poorer

IV. In Sickness and In Health

V. To Love and to Cherish

VI. 'Til Death Do Us Part

I. To Have and To Hold

The End   The Beginning

All of my life I had wanted to be like Cinderella and to live happily ever after with my prince. That was not to be. Instead of a crown, I was left with ashes. Instead of beauty, I was left with sickness. Instead of a castle-home, I was left with ruins. My heart was broken and my life dethroned. All I had left was my Lord. Nothing else. I thought of the poem by Robert Frost, "Two roads diverged in a wood, and I – I took the one less traveled by, and that has made all the difference." I had a choice for I was standing at the crossroads and I had to choose which road to take. *"This is what the Lord says: Stand at the crossroads and look; ask for the ancient paths, ask where the good way is, and walk in it, and you will find rest for your souls."* (Jeremiah 6:16) Rest. That was what I needed. So, I chose to take the road less traveled. *"But small is the gate and narrow the road that leads to life, and only a few find it."* (Matthew 7:13) With this thought, my heart began to mend. God had made me for a purpose. I would travel this road with Him for if only a few find it, this road must be filled with rare gifts and treasures. *"Call to me and I will answer you and tell you great and unsearchable things you do not know."* (Jeremiah 33:3) I called to Him and He took my hand with His righteous right hand and we began our journey. This road was narrow, untraveled, yet beautiful. The more I walked with Him, the more beautiful I became for He had bestowed upon me *"a crown of beauty instead of ashes."* (Isaiah 61:3) My motto became, "Making beauty out of ashes." God had given me a rare gift – His gift of beauty. I thanked Him daily for that "unsearchable treasure." My Cinderella wish had come true. I, who had lived among the ashes, had been restored to the throne of Grace by my Lord – the Prince of Peace. Not only had I been given beauty but I had been given rest. Trust Him. Place your broken heart into His strong and loving hands. He will bestow upon you, "a crown of beauty instead of ashes." And, like Cinderella, who lived among the ashes, you too will be escorted to the throne by this great and mighty prince who loves you more than life.

Rejected   Loved

The pain of being rejected is overpowering. *"I am forced to restore what I did not steal."* (Psalm 69:4) My heart is broken and, yes, I am forced to restore even that. I cling to your words, *"The Lord will call you back as if you were a wife deserted and distressed in spirit –a wife who married young only to be rejected."* (Isaiah 54:6) Thank you Lord for understanding me completely, and for your direction. *"Forget the former things: do not dwell on the past. See I am doing a new thing! Now it springs up; do you not perceive it? I am making a way in the wasteland.* (Isaiah 43:18 & 19) *"For I know the plans I have for you declares the Lord, plans to prosper you and not to harm you, plans to give you a hope and a future."* (Jeremiah 29:11) And so, my new life begins. I am loved, not for a while, but forever.

Forgotten   Summoned

"Fear not, for I have redeemed you; I have summoned you by name, you are mine. When you pass through the waters, I will be with you; and when you pass through the rivers, they will not sweep over you. When you walk through the fire, you will not be burned; the flames will not set you ablaze. For I am the Lord your God." (Isaiah 43:1-3) I wept when I read these words from the Lord. The struggle on this earth had been so excruciating and hopeless, but He was promising to be with me through it all. Even though the rivers and flames were there, I would not be consumed. He gave me hope and I knew that I must cling to Him for He loved me more than life itself. He had called me by name. He claimed me as His and in return gave himself to me.

I have wept many times over this passage and weep even now as I write. I am still amazed at His love for me and how He cares for every detail in my life. Thank you Lord for the greatest love that I have ever known.

Broken   **Mended**

Tonight I have awakened again. I am lonely and so intensely feel the broken pieces of my heart. Speak to me Lord. Help me feel your love. *"The Lord your God is with you, He is mighty to save. He will take great delight in you, He will quiet you with his love, He will rejoice over you with singing."* (Zephaniah 3:17) Thank you for your word, your beauty and your peace. *"I will lie down and sleep for you alone, O Lord make me dwell in safety."* (Psalm 4:8)

Lost   Gathered

I am alone in this house with my children. I am their everything now. I feel overwhelmed – incompetent. *"He tends his flock like a shepherd: He gathers the lambs in his arms and carries them close to His heart; He gently leads those that have young."* (Isaiah 40:11) I am so grateful Lord for the release of this burden. You know it is too much for me to bear. You carry us close to your heart. Now, I weep because I am overwhelmed by your great love wrapped in gentle tenderness. You are our everything. I am not alone. I will rest in your arms.

Honey and Green Clay Facial Mask

"Create in me a pure heart, God, and renew a steadfast spirit within me." Psalm 51:10

1 teaspoon of green clay

1 teaspoon of honey

Mix together in a bowl and apply directly to the face – covering well. (You will want to pull your hair back.) Set your timer for 15 minutes. Use this time to thank the Lord for using this facial mask to purify your face while He purifies your heart.

II. For Better, For Worse

Destruction **Victory**

Will this ever end Lord? *"Not a word from their mouth can be trusted, their heart is filled with destruction. Their throat is an open grave; with their tongue they speak deceit."* (Psalm 5:9) I am drained from this oppression. I need your strength. *"The sorrows for the appointed feasts I will remove from you; they are a burden and a reproach to you."* (Zephaniah 3:18-20)   Thank you Lord for this promise and for knowing the truth. So many people cannot see all of this ugliness, but you Lord know all things. I will rest in your promise.

Confusion   Direction

Lord, I cry out to you for direction. I do not know what step to take next. There seems to be no blueprint available for this life of heartache and confusion. Lead me Lord. *"How gracious He will be when you cry for help! As soon as He hears, He will answer you. Although the Lord gives you the bread of adversity and the water of affliction, your teachers will be hidden no more; with your own eyes you will see them. Whether you turn to the right or to the left, your ears will hear a voice behind you, saying, 'This is the way, walk in it.'"* (Isaiah 30:19-21) O Lord, thank you for the direction that you have given to me in this time of difficulty. You have placed your people of wisdom before me. I praise you for my church and for the elders whose hearts have been opened to me. Only you Lord could have given them this understanding. And through you Lord, I am finding rest for my soul.

"This is what the Lord says: Stand at the crossroads and look; ask for the ancient paths, ask where the good way is, and walk in it, and you will find rest for your souls." (Jeremiah 6:16) Thank you Lord for this rest.

Deceit   Truth

"Let this people turn to you, but you must not turn to them. I will make you a wall to this people, a fortified wall of bronze; they will fight against you but will not overcome you, for I am with you to rescue and save you, declares the Lord. I will save you from the hands of the wicked and redeem you from the grasp of the cruel." (Jeremiah 15:19-21) This was one of the hardest commands given to me by the Lord. I had always "turned" wanting to fix everything. Consequently, my compassionate heart became a hindrance and a tool of destruction towards myself. The harder I tried, the deeper I fell into the pit of depression and hurt. The battle, I realized, was too big for me. It belonged to my Almighty God. As I daily began to apply His precepts, my eyes were opened to the truth. Things I had previously been unable to see, now unfolded before me. As I stood back and let go, I saw the wickedness and cruelty. I was so thankful that I had followed His direction.

Only He could save me and rescue me. And, I knew that He wanted this place in my life. The greatest honor I could give to Him was to release this burden and trust Him. Thank you Lord for being my Savior, my husband, and my friend. *"Greater love has no one than this, that he lay down his life for his friends. You are my friends if you do what I command. I no longer call you servants, because a servant does not know his maker's business. Instead I have called you friends for everything that I learned from my Father I have made known to you."* (John 15:13-15)

Guilty   Redeemed

"Though your sins are like scarlet, they shall be as white as snow; though they are red as crimson, they shall be like wool." (Isaiah 1:18b) O Lord, I feel so unworthy of your presence. Forgive me.

"I do not understand what I do. For what I want to do I do not do, but what I hate I do." (Romans 7:15) Everyday Lord, I long to please you yet I stumble. Then, the guilt consumes me. It reels over and over in my head during the long and silent darkness of the night. I search the scriptures and there is your answer for me. *"Therefore, there is now no condemnation for those who are in Christ Jesus."* (Romans 8:1) Thank you Father for your grace and for your compassion. *"As a father has compassion on his children, so the Lord has compassion on those who fear Him; for He knows how we are formed, He remembers that we are dust."* (Psalm 103:13-14) You have promised that you will redeem me *"and without money you will be redeemed"*

(Isaiah 52:3) How could I ever repay you? I can't Lord, for that is your gift of grace. Not only am I forgiven, I have been redeemed. *"Praise the Lord, O my soul, and forget not all his benefits – who forgives all your sins and heals all your diseases, who redeems your life from the pit and crowns you with love and compassion, who satisfies your desires with good things so that your youth is renewed like the eagle's."* (Psalm 103:2-5)

Olive Oil Foot Scrub

"Now that I, your Lord and Teacher, have washed your feet, you also should wash one another's feet."
John 13:14

Pour olive oil into the palm of your hand. Add sea salt to the oil. Gently scrub your feet with the oil mixture. Allow to penetrate, and then rinse. This treatment increases circulation and softens the feet. Think of Jesus lovingly washing your feet.

III. For Richer, For Poorer

Deficient Faith

O Lord, I do not know how I am going to make it every month on this salary. So many bills Lord, and so many needs. On paper, this situation looks impossible. My bills exceed my salary but I know you will provide. You have placed me in this home and it is yours. All things are yours Lord and with you *"all things are possible."* I am going to trust you Lord. I am going to believe for your word says, *"Have faith in God,"* Jesus answered. *"I tell you, whatever you ask for in prayer, believe that you have received it, and it will be yours."*

(Mark 11:22-24) Thank you Lord for being my provider.

Worry   Provision

"Therefore I tell you, do not worry about your life, what you will eat or drink; or about your body, what you will wear. Is not life more important than clothes? Look at the birds of the air; they do not sow or reap or store away in barns, and yet your heavenly Father feeds them. Are you not much more valuable than they?" (Matthew 6:25-26) *"But seek first his kingdom and his righteousness, and all these things will be given to you as well."* (Matthew 6:33) How many times God has proven His love and His stamp of value on my life through His tender care and provision. So many blessings have been literally dropped down from heaven. I have stepped on money, found money in my pocket, received money in my mailbox, and been issued unexpected money from my job.

God owns the cattle on a thousand hills. *"For every animal of the forest is mine, and the cattle on a thousand hills."* (Psalm 50:10) Everything is His. God will supply our needs for He is faithful. I thank you Lord for how valuable I am to you, and that I do not have to worry.

Destitute   Blessings

"Bring the whole tithe into the storehouse that there may be food in my house. Test me in this, says the Lord Almighty and see if I will not open the floodgates of heaven and pour out so much blessing that you will not have enough room for it." (Malachi 3:10) God has proven Himself so faithful in this promise. So many times He has miraculously provided for us. Though it is not easy financially as a single mother, we have never lacked. "Test me," He says. You will find that His promise is true. I am so thankful for His provision – His showers of blessings. What a privilege it is to give to Him.

Afflicted   Favored

Another difficult situation. A broken home has many troubles. It is constantly attacked by anger, resentment, and pain. It is so hard to raise children in this world and even more so in a broken family. *"Relent, O Lord! How long will it be? Have compassion on your servants.*
Satisfy us in the morning with your unfailing love, that we may sing for joy and be glad all our days. Make us glad for as many days as you have afflicted us, for as many years as we have seen trouble. May your deeds be shown to your servants, your splendor to their children. May the favor of the Lord our God rest upon us; establish the work of our hands for us -yes, establish the work of our hands." (Psalm 90:13-17) Thank you Lord for these encouraging words. I will continue to work at this job with pleasure, for you have promised your favor upon me. You have established the work of my hands and for that I am grateful.

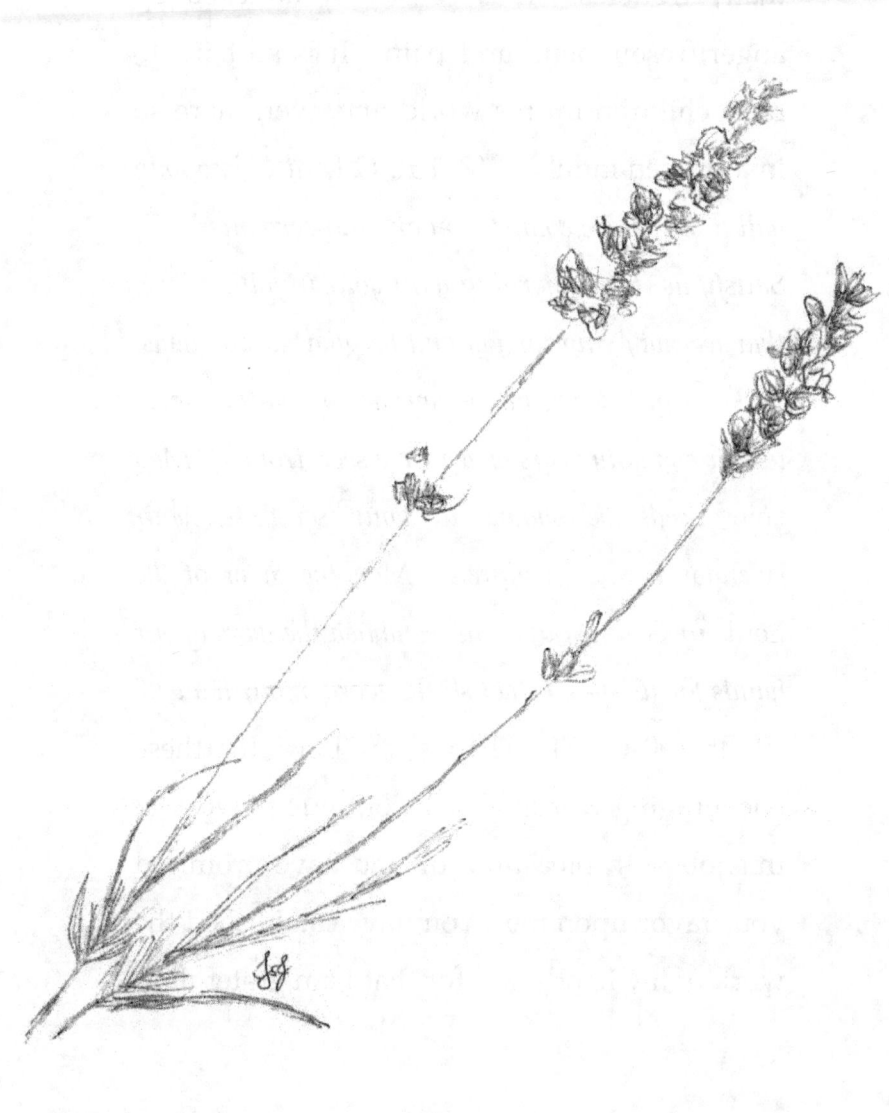

Cloves and Lavender-The Perfect Bath
God's perfect number

4 oil drops of cloves
3 oil drops of lavender

Add your 7 drops while filling your bath. I love to think on God's perfect number while soaking in this sweet smelling bath. You may want to add a little olive oil. The oil of cloves can be very strong and irritating if in direct contact with the skin. This bath is very cleansing for the clove is a natural antiseptic while the lavender is very beneficial for the skin.

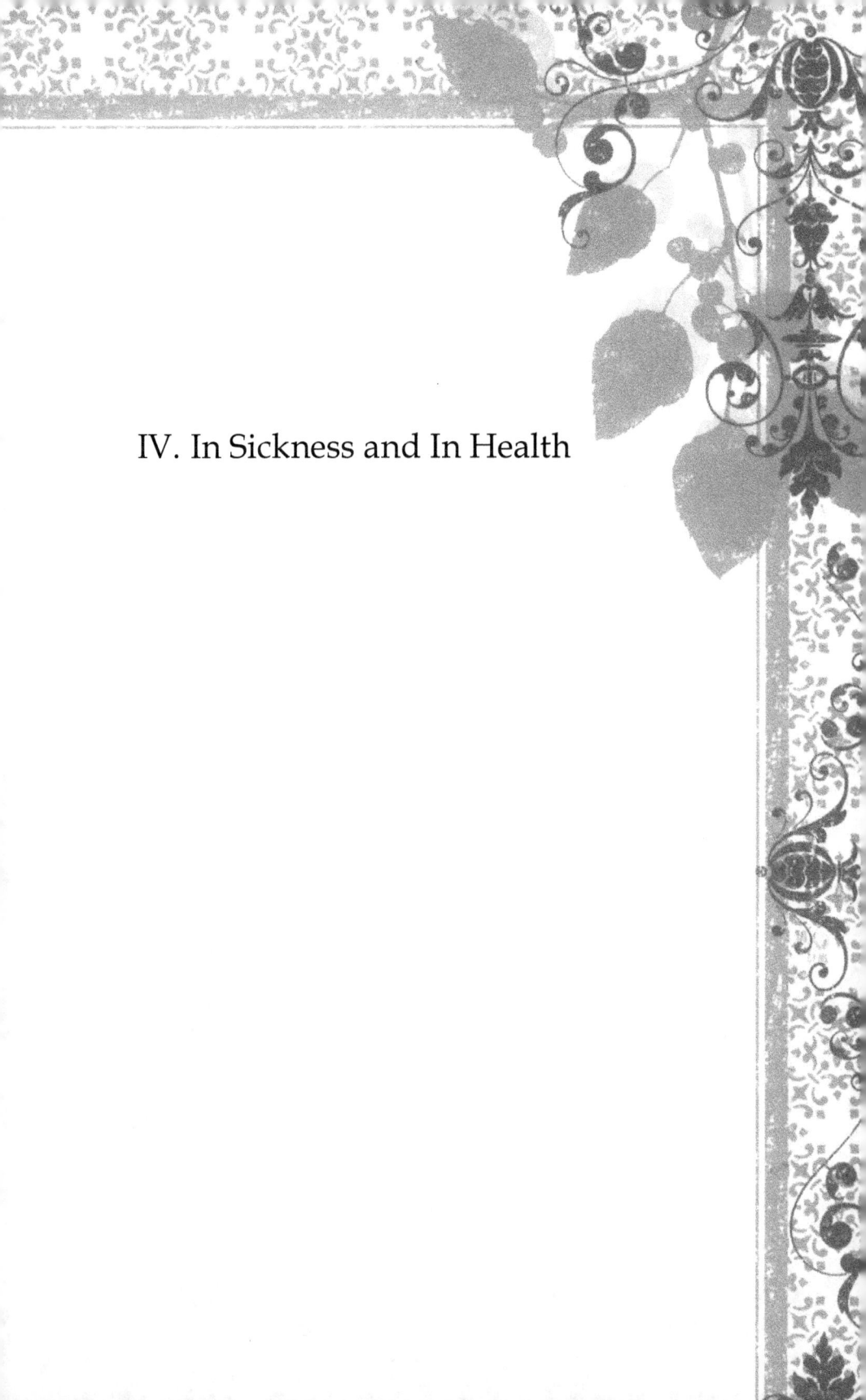

IV. In Sickness and In Health

Pain   Trust

"Trust in the Lord with all your heart and lean not on your own understanding. In all your ways acknowledge Him, and He will make your paths straight." (Proverbs 3:5-6) O Lord, this pain is unbearable and this sickness is debilitating. I am unable to be a mother, and I thought that was my calling. I am unable to go to work Lord, and I am now the provider of this little family. I am unable to go home but perhaps you are preparing me to go home with you. How can I leave my children, Lord? Who will love them like I do? I know Lord. You love them more than I ever could and in that I must trust. You know that I cannot understand this, so you are telling me not to. Direct my path, Lord even though I cannot walk now. Direct me while I lie here. I am yours and I give all that I have to you.

Dying   **Healing**

The words of the doctor reeled in my head, "You need to have surgery but you will not make it through another one now." I knew I would not as well. "God," I prayed, "is this it for me, or am I to recover only to have a third surgery?" I knew in my heart that I would not live through it this time. In my agony, I heard a still small voice penetrate within me, *"A righteous man may have many troubles, but the Lord delivers him from them all; He protects all his bones, not one of them will be broken."* (Psalm 34:19-20) There was my hope. I must believe. Everyday, I quoted these verses. I wrote them, posted them, and meditated upon them. My God had spoken to me and though the circumstances looked impossible, He had made a promise. I wept with tears of relief and hope. My healing began, one beautiful day at a time.

Thank you Lord that with you, "All things are possible." (Matthew 19:26) We have had many years of trouble, but you have promised to make us glad for as many years as we have suffered. I believe Lord. I thank you for your favor and I will look daily for your splendor.

Pillaged   Renowned

Although my family has scars and wounds, you Lord, have given us hope, joy, and beauty. *"You will go out in joy and be led forth in peace; the mountains and hills will burst in song before you, and all the trees of the field will clap their hands. Instead of the thornbush will grow the pinetree, and instead of briers the myrtle will grow. This will be the Lord's renown, for an everlasting sign, which will not be destroyed."* (Isaiah 55:12-13) Thank you Lord, for the beauty that you bring into my life. *"The Lord will guide you always; he will satisfy your needs in a sun-scorched land and will strengthen your frame. You will be like a well-watered garden, like a spring whose waters never fail."* (Isaiah 58:11)

Fear   Power

Fear, I realized, had become a constant companion of mine. When seemingly everything had been taken away and I felt I was left with nothing, God became my strength. Little by little, I came to trust Him more and to fear less. I continuously declared His sovereignty in my life and hung on to His promise that all things work for good to those who love him. *"And we know that in all things God works for the good of those who love him, who have been called according to his purpose."* (Romans 8:28) My fear began to be replaced with His power, *"For God did not give us a spirit of timidity, but a spirit of power, of love and of self-discipline."* (2 Timothy 1:7) Ah, the freedom that comes from living in His strength. I praise you for, *"The joy of the Lord is my strength."* (Nehemiah 8:10)

Olive Oil Exfoliate

"But I am like an olive tree flourishing in the house of God; I trust in God's unfailing love for ever and ever." Psalm 52:8

Fill your tub with warm water. Generously apply olive oil all over your body. Using a sea sponge, gently scrub your body. This will open your pores and will enable the olive oil to soak in your skin. Meditate on Jesus walking among the Olive trees and along the Dead Sea. You will feel invigorated, cleansed and moisturized.

*If you have tired muscles and need to relax after the scrub, add salts to your bath and soak. Rest in Him.

V. To Love and To Cherish

Trying to love again -

The journey that took me to the other side

When I hugged him
It was not the same
You were greater

When I looked in his eyes
It wasn't the same
You were worthier

When I went to him for comfort
It wasn't the same
You were mightier

He had lost to You

I longed for the physical touch
But each time
It was never the same
You were always there

He could see
In my eyes
It wasn't the same

The Lover –

In my heart
Forever

"Place me like a seal over your heart,
like a seal on your arm;
for love is as strong as death,
its jealousy unyielding as the grave,
It burns like a blazing fire,
like a mighty flame.
Many waters cannot quench love;
rivers cannot wash it away.
If one were to give
all the wealth of his house for love,
it would be utterly scorned."

Song of Songs 8:6-7

Deserted   Claimed

"*For your maker is your husband the Lord Almighty is His name.*" (Jeremiah 2:1) Today, I can begin my new life with you Lord for you know my deepest thoughts and desires – my past, my present and my future. "*I remember the devotion of your youth, how as a young bride you loved me and followed me through the desert through a land not sown.*" (Jeremiah 2: 2) I do not ever need to be afraid again for you Lord will always protect me and you are always faithful.

Lavender and Peppermint Facial Sauna

"Live a life of love, just as Christ loved us and gave himself up for us as a fragrant offering"
Ephesians 5:2

3 Cups of distilled water
1 Tablespoon of lavender leaves
1 Tablespoon of peppermint leaves
Cover and bring to a boil

Take pot of boiling herbs to your table, place on a hot plate and set your timer for 15 minutes. Place a large towel over your head and breathe in this soothing aroma. The steam is very hot so open the lid gradually during your 15-minute therapy time. The lavender will bring calmness and relief from stress while peppermint brings refreshment. The lavender is also excellent for the skin. These facial saunas have become a wonderful prayer time for me - a time of beauty from ashes.

*After your facial, pour the lavender/peppermint through a strainer and into your bath water.

VI. 'Til Death Do Us Part

Anguish   Hope

"My heart is in anguish within me; the terrors of death assail me. Fear and trembling have beset me; horror has overwhelmed me. I said, 'Oh that I had the wings of a dove! I would fly away and be at rest– I would flee far away and stay in the desert; I would hurry to my place of shelter, far from the tempest and storm.' If an enemy were insulting me, I could endure it; if a foe were raising himself against me, I could hide from him. But it is you, a man like myself, my companion, my close friend, with whom I once enjoyed sweet fellowship as we walked with the throng at the house of God. My companion attacks his friends; he violates his covenant. His speech is smooth as butter, yet war is in his heart; his words are more soothing than oil, yet they are drawn swords." (Psalm 55:20-21)

Rejection. Lord, you know. You understand. Help me through this extremely devastating time of my life. There is no one who understands the depth of this but you. Thank you Lord for this comfort. *"Cast your cares on the Lord and he will sustain you; he will never let the righteous fall."* (Psalm 55:20-22)

Crushed   **Delivered**

"I will bring him near and he will come close to me, for who is he who will devote himself to me? declares the Lord." (Jeremiah 30:21) I long to be close to you, Lord. I need your nearness for my heart is crushed. I have come. Bring me near. Deliver me, for I am devoted to you.

"The Lord is close to the brokenhearted and saves those who are crushed in spirit." (Psalm 34:18)

Abandoned   Established

"I will bring them back to this place and let them live in safety. They will be my people and I will be their God. I will give them singleness of heart and action, so that they will always fear me for their own good and the good of their children after them. I will make an everlasting covenant with them: I will never stop doing good to them, and I will inspire them to fear me, so that they will never turn away from me. I will rejoice in doing them good and will assuredly plant them in this land with all my heart and soul." (Jeremiah 32:37-41) O Lord, I am amazed that you express your love so deeply. Thank you for bringing me back and establishing me in this land. I love you, Lord. Thank you for giving me singleness of heart.

Ruins   Restoration

"I have loved you with an everlasting love; I have drawn you with loving-kindness. I will build you up again and you will be rebuilt, O Virgin Israel. Again you will take up your tambourines, and go out and dance with the joyful." (Jeremiah 31: 3-4) By these words Lord, I know I am truly loved with an everlasting love and that you know the secret desires of my heart. I will take up my tambourine. I will dance again with the joyful! I praise you for the hope that fills my heart.

Ashes   Beauty

"In that day – Sing about a fruitful vineyard; I the Lord, watch over it; I water it continually. I guard it day and night so that no one may harm it." (Isaiah 27:3) Today I planted flowers and I hung a flag with this verse on it. I stand amazed at God's beauty in the midst of these sorrows. His beauty feels like sunny rain on this dark, dry land. I will make beauty out of ashes Lord, for you have given me that desire. You are the Master Creator and I long to be like you. I will daily soak in your beauty and continuously think on your lovely things. *"Whatever is true, whatever is noble, whatever is right, whatever is pure, whatever is lovely, whatever is admirable – if anything is excellent or praiseworthy – think about such things."* (Philippians 4:8)

Beauty   Splendor

"To bestow on them a crown of beauty instead of ashes, the oil of gladness instead of mourning, and a garment of praise instead of a spirit of despair. They will be called oaks of righteousness, a planting of the Lord for the display of His splendor." (Isaiah 61:3) O Lord, you have given me a crown of beauty and I thank you. My heart is full of hope for the things to come. You planted me here and this is where I will bloom. *"The Lord will surely comfort Zion and will look with compassion on all her ruins; He will make her deserts like Eden, her wastelands like the garden of the Lord. Joy and gladness will be found in her; thanksgiving and the sound of singing."* (Isaiah 51:3) And now Lord, I must go and share this beauty. *"I will tell of the kindness of the Lord, the deeds for which He is to be praised, according to all the Lord has done for us – yes, the many good things He has done."* (Isaiah 63:7)

Epilogue

"The nations will see your righteousness, and all kings your glory; you will be called by a new name that the mouth of the Lord will bestow.

You will be called a crown of splendor in the Lord's hand, a royal diadem in the hand of the Lord.

No longer will they call you Deserted, or name your land Desolate. But you will be called Hephzibah (my delight is in her), and your land Beulah (married); for the Lord will take delight in you."

Isaiah 62:2-4

With every end, comes a new beginning.
Begin your new life with His first promise:

He raises the poor from the dust and lifts the needy from the ash heap; He seats them with princes, with their princes of their people.
Psalm 113:7-8

www.ingramcontent.com/pod-product-compliance
Lightning Source LLC
Chambersburg PA
CBHW050605300426
44112CB00013B/2077